The Essent

CW00566070

Vespa
SCOOTERS
Classic two-stroke models
1960 to 2008

Your marque expert:
Mark Paxton

VELOCE PUBLISHING
THE PUBLISHER OF FINE AUTOMOTIVE BOOKS

www.veloce.co.uk

For post publication news, updates and amendments relating to this book please visit www.veloce.co.uk/books/V4883

First published in September 2010 by Veloce Publishing Limited, Veloce House, Parkway Farm Business Park, Middle Farm Way, Poundbury, Dorchester, Dorset, DT1 3AR, England. Updated & revised edition February 2016.
Fax 01305 250479/e-mail info@veloce.co.uk/web www.veloce.co.uk or www.velocebooks.com.

Introduction
– the purpose of this book

Introduction

The two-stroke Vespa is a unique vehicle, recognised by automotive historians as a design classic, thanks to avant garde construction techniques, like monocoque frames, combined with innovative styling and compact power units. That recognition extends to the public, too, who are aware it's not only a symbol of its native country, Italy, but also of sun, fun and youthful exuberance. Also appreciating the Vespa's charms are those lucky owners, past and present, who have relied on its dogged dependability whilst revelling in its stylish looks, and a level of enjoyment unrivalled by any of the competition. With such a wide appeal, it's unsurprising that demand is at an all time high and values are rising.

Two-stroke Vespas are still willing work-horses.

The downside of this popularity is that care has to be exercised when buying a classic Vespa to avoid the duds, hastily spruced up to make a quick profit. That's where where this book comes in. It makes no pretence at being a history of the marque, or a spotters guide to the dozens of variants produced by Piaggio. Instead, it concentrates on ensuring that the newcomer to the world of classic Vespas is aware of the potential pitfalls. Before making a start on your search for a new machine, read through the book in full, to gain an overview. Then, when examining a potential purchase, take the book with you, and use the points system to help decide.

It may seem a little dispiriting to read about all the potential flaws, but don't despair; two-stroke Vespas, in general, are tough and reliable, (many PXs, for example, are still puttering around as daily work-horses for the Spanish Post Office). There shouldn't be too many that you look at suffering badly from the listed malaises. Find a good one, and the rewards are immense; not just the pleasure derived from owning and riding it, but also the knowledge that, looked after, it will hold its value, unlike a modern scooter. Who, after all, could resist the thought of their own little peice of La Dolce Vita sitting on the driveway?

Please note

The scooters covered in this book fall into two clear categories; large frame (VBB, Sprint, Rally, PX for example) and were 125cc and over (although 80 and 100cc PXs were sold on the Continent), and small frame which, as the name suggests, are smaller and only sold in capacities from 50cc up to 125cc. Apart from the engine difference, the two lines are very similar in design and construction. Any specific differences when buying are noted in the text. Finally, if left and right are mentioned, that orientation is based on the rider sitting astride the scooter facing forward.

Essential Buyer's Guide™ currency

At the time of publication a BG unit of currency "●" equals approximately £1.00/US$1.51/Euro 1.38. Please adjust to suit current exchange rates using Sterling as the base currency.

Contents

1 Is it the right scooter for you?
– marriage guidance

Tall and short riders
Seat heights in general are reasonably low, but the stretch across the footboards to get your feet on the ground adds inches. A small frame may be a better option for shorter riders and, perhaps, some lady enthusists. Legroom is fine on the large frames, even for those in excess of 6 feet (1.83 metre).

Weight of controls
Clutches should have a light pull if the cable is in good condition. The gear change should move easily, although it can feel imprecise and a little awkward, until you get used to it. The throttle should match the clutch for ease of movement. If not, then the cable needs lubrication or replacement. Getting maximum throttle movement can take an irritating second handful, and the return-spring can sometimes be a bit weak. Vespas fitted with front drums need a good pull on the lever to get the most out of the brake; disc-equipped versions are more powerful. Rear brakes can seem a little insensitive at first, but you'll soon get accustomed to how your particular scooter reacts.

Dimensions
	Weight	Length	Width
PX125	97kg (213lb)	1.81m (71in)	74cm (29.1in)
Sprint 150	89kg (195lb)	1.77m (69.6in)	67cm (26.3in)
Primavera	73kg (160lb)	1.66m (65.6in)	67cm (26.3in

Comfort
Far superior to any motorbike, with better weather protection thanks to the legshields and good wheel enclosure. Seats are comfy, too: earlier spring versions are often preferred to the later type. Many enthusiasts use their Vespas for long distance travel, and have done for decades.

Running costs
One of the cheapest forms of motorised transport. Good fuel consumption, cheap parts and repairs, low tyre wear, low road tax; the benefits go on and on.

Sample fuel consumption figures, from road tests and rider reports, as well as some factory figures, are listed in Chapter 17.

PX125	85mpg (Imperial gallon)	30km/l
PX200	65mpg	23km/l
150 Sprint	90mpg	32km/l
Primavera	90mpg	32km/l
50 Special	115mpg	40km/l

Usability
Vespas are nippy and nimble around city streets; attributes which, if anything, are even more useful on today's congested roads than they were when originally produced.

The PX range; easiest to live with, and the most common.

Parts availability
Superb. Many original bits are still made by Piaggio, there are hundreds of aftermarket suppliers, and new parts are arriving almost daily to plug any gaps in the market. If you're buying a mainstream model from the period covered by this book, virtually everything to keep it on the road will be readily available.

Parts cost
Low. Most items are very reasonably priced. A Vespa can be bought and enjoyed by those on a very tight budget.

Parts quality
This is an area where caution should be exercised. In general, the advice is to go for factory parts, if you can afford them. Alternatively, use a quality supplier who sources items from the EEC. Consider items from outside Europe only as a last resort, though be aware of potential quality issues.

Insurance group
If you're using your Vespa purely for leisure, try to get classic insurance; the mileage may be limited but you'll get an agreed value and, perhaps, salvage retention rights. If yours is a more modern scooter, such as a PX, and you'll be using it for commuting, then the insurance group varies from company to company. As a guide, though, a PX125 will be between three and six (UK) and a PX200 between six and nine.

Investment potential
Rare models are likely to increase in value as time passes; more mainstream ones are probably going to hold their value as long as condition is maintained.

Foibles
Suspension can be bouncy on the front, and there's limited travel on the back. Anything pre-PX can suffer from a disconcerting amount of nose-dive under braking. There's also the issue of mixing two-stroke oil in the fuel on non-autolube scooters.

Minus points
Can be slow for their capacity, compared to motorbikes. They can also suffer from vibration, and are often criticised for their handling; but this latter issue is something you'll get used to.

Alternatives
The only likely alternatives are newer Vespas (automatics and without the period charm of the originals), or Lambrettas, which offer a similar experience but are generally regarded as less reliable, although may offer better roadholding.

2 Cost considerations
– affordable, or a money pit?

Vespa parts are relatively inexpensive, however some aftermarket pieces do not match the quality of the originals. Ask club mates for recommendations, and don't forget your local scooter shop, which should be fully aware of any problem parts. Service prices vary across regions, so expect to pay more in large cities. The prices below are the minimum for quality parts for the most popular models; older and rarer variants will obviously cost more.

Small service ●x60
Large service ●x110
Brake drum ●x40
Brake shoes ●x12
Brake caliper ●x70
Brake disc ●x30
Brake pads ●x10
Exhaust ●x55
Engine, new (LML) ●x700
Piston and barrel ●x125
Crankshaft ●x100
Con rod kit ●x45

Clutch (complete, later type) ●x125
Clutch plates ●x18
Cable set ●x22
Headlight ●x35
Coil (CDI unit) ●x30
Stator plate ●x65
Points and condenser ●x15
Carburettor ●x70
Jets ●x4
Air filter ●x16
Floor repair section ●x38
Seat ●x75

Parts that are hard to find
Unique parts for short production run models of all sizes, and genuine trim for older models. Also, some Femsa ignition bits, over-size pistons for older engines, and UK market Sportique bits that differ from Italian VBB.

Parts that are expensive
Period accessories for that perfect restoration, genuine engines, plus all the hard to find bits above.

Spares are reasonably priced – even electronic parts.

Any Vespa two-stroke will undoubtedly add a certain charisma and style to even the most mundane journey. But there are occasions where the reality of modern road conditions can intrude on that charm. A 50cc small frame, for example, will be a frustrating ride. With its asthmatic acceleration and inability to crack 30mph, it would make a poor choice, unless you were legally limited to that capacity by age. Anything from 125cc upwards is fine around town, and for local trips. If long distance rallies and tours are your thing, then a 200cc engine might be more suitable. The cost difference between

Any model can be used, but over 125cc is preferable for long-distance travel.

The back end looks symmetrical, but the engine hangs off the right-hand side.

capacities is not sufficiently great to be a major disincentive, so go for the one that best suits your intended use. Performance levels for all the scooters covered in this book are lower than you might imagine. Piaggio were serious about reliability, so standard tune engines are limited, by a combination of porting and exhaust configuration, to prevent over revving. This also helps produce very good fuel consumption figures for this type of motor. Tuning is obviously an option, if you are determined to go faster, but carries potential reliability penalties unless carried out well. If outright speed is truly a concern, then a modern, four-stroke Vespa might be a better choice (although they lack the same charm).

Road holding and handling are often called in to question on scooters in general, with the Vespa, in particular, being accused of an inherent imbalance (due to the weight of the right-hand side mounted motor). Indeed, care should be taken the first time you roll one off its centre-stand; it could catch you unawares. Once on the road, the reality is rather different: your riding style almost immediately compensates for any lop-sidedness, and you'll be hard pushed to find a regular rider who complains of it. Like engine performance, handling was steadily improved with each successive model, and the P series is really very good. Handling can be further enhanced by fitting modern tyres, which have better treads and stickier compounds.

Comfort levels are high – far better than traditional two wheelers. There's plenty of legroom (both fore-and-aft, and side-to-side), although two-up it becomes a little more cramped. Seats are comfy for a couple of hours, with the earlier steel-sprung versions being the best. Suspension travel is fine, if a little soggy, but avoid potholes; those small wheels drop into them rather too easily. Controls are light and easy to master but braking from the drum setup is now a bit outdated, so you need to give yourself a few extra feet just in case (later disc-equipped versions are fine).

Maintenance is straightforward, with the DIY enthusiast able to address most issues, once armed with an appropriate manual. Weekend tinkering is both very rewarding, and a great way to get to know your scooter. Repair prices are low (even if the job is handed over to a shop) as the motor is simple, accessible and well laid out. Parts are plentiful and readily available, so down-time shouldn't be a problem in the event of a mechanical disaster. As long as care is taken to prevent rust taking hold and spreading, these classic Vespas can be kept going almost indefinitely. Any financial input will be rewarded with very low depreciation rates, and even the possibility of rising values on some versions. Chuck an active social and club scene into the overall equation, and the appeal is pretty much unequalled.

Two-up can be a little cramped.

These may all be sensible reasons to buy a classic Vespa, but tend to pale into insignificance, as most buyers today want something with character as a weekend treat. This is where the older models score most highly. With their cleaner lines, uncluttered by indicators and clumpy tail lights, many potential owners are willing to sacrifice a little ease of use in order to have the coolest set of wheels in the neighbourhood.

The combination, then, of initial cost, style, reliability, charisma and genuine iconic and historic status should make owning a two-stroke, geared Vespa a pleasure – just make sure that you buy the right one to begin with!

Older models make ideal weekend pleasure machines.

4 Relative values
– which model for you?

This chapter shows relative values of individual models, in good working order and cosmetic condition. Expressed as a percentage, the value is based on a combination of recent dealer prices and private sales. Changes in fashion, or increasing rarity, mean the models can – and do – move relative to one another, so check the internet, or magazine small ads for recent trends.

SS90
Top of the tree for value, thanks to a combination of its rarity and period sporting success. With cut-down legshields, narrow, dropped-bars and centrally mounted, vertical spare-wheel (topped with a fake tank, which is actually a tool box), it's a striking scooter. One to collect, rather than ride, as comparable performance is available in cheaper, more readily available models. Make sure the frame and engine numbers are correct for the model, as copies and fakes aren't uncommon. In Europe, there was a 50cc version, also highly prized.
100%

The SS90 is highly sought-after, with prices to match.

GS160 MK 1/2

Beautifully styled, fast, but thirsty. The first incarnation had a small toolbox, accessible from above the rear tail light. On the second series, this was replaced by a legshield toolbox. Sought after model, especially in the UK, so like the SS90, make sure the scooter you're buying is genuine.
95%

RALLY 180/200

Another favourite in the UK and Europe. The replacement for the SS180, it was finally fitted with rotary valve technology, and the styling 'updated', with plastic starting to replace alloy trim. The 200 was equipped with electronic ignition, and even autolube as an option in some markets. Fast, reliable and stylish.
80%

The Rally is a great scooter, and still usable today.

SS180

Designed to replace the GS. Although the SS180 was still a reasonably nippy scooter, the piston-ported engine was starting to show signs of its age, and the refreshed styling, complete with the trapezoid headlight, did little to increase its appeal at the time. A short life span, and associated rarity, help to boost values.
80%

The SS180; the last of the piston-ported Vespas, and rapidly rising in value.

PX200

Pretty much identical to the PX125/150, but with a larger engine, and blessed with electronic ignition from the start (the smaller models had to wait four years before losing their points setup).The most useful day-to-day scooter, with good performance and acceptable fuel consumption.

40%

VBB

The beginnings of the 'new Vespa'. A rotary valve intake (where fuel was metered by the crank, rather than by the piston) allowed a far leaner two-stroke mix, giving better economy and performance. Great styling, with curvaceous panel work, the VBB has four ratios (one up from its predecessor), but still runs on 8 inch wheels. Many are converted to 10 inch wheels, when a later engine is slotted-in.

35% (GL and Douglas Sportique plus 5%)

Original '60s VBBs are becoming rare.

T5

Basically, a sports PX125 fitted with a five-port engine. producing as much power as the PX200. Early models' styling is generally regarded as unappealing, whilst the later Classic followed PX lines.

30%

PX125/150

The most common Vespa two-stroke for sale today. It was a major step forward, with better electrics, stronger engines, improved handling, and increased reliability. The only downside is the rather clunky styling. Plenty around, so be choosy. Late, low-mileage ones hold their price well.

30%

**The T5 Mark 1
was fast, and stood
out from the crowd.**

The 125 Primavera is a great town scooter; nimble and nippy.

SPRINT
Basically a replacement for the GL. With 10 inch wheels, decent trim, and reasonable performance, it was a good seller, and remains popular today. Styling is more angular than earlier scooters, but still attractive. The trapezoid headlamp, from its predecessor, was kept to differentiate it from the cheaper Super.
28%

PRIMAVERA
Many regard the Primavera as the best of the small frame range. A large number were produced, so some are still around. It offers the best balance of performance, economy and road holding. The rarer ET3 was even quicker.
25% (plus 10% for ET3)

SUPER
A lower specification Sprint, running on 8 inch rims. The engine is a two-port design, which is reliable, if unexciting. A single-seat and luggage rack were fitted in some markets.
20%

Other small frames
These are pretty much the same, in value terms. The last-of-the-line PKs, though, are probably worth the least, as their styling is pretty much universally disliked.
20% (PK less 5%)

5 Before you buy
– be well informed

Before you begin the hunt for your dream scooter, visit a few dealers and familiarise yourself with how a scooter should look. What do the controls feel like? How strong is the compression as you push down on the kickstart? How bouncy is the suspension? New LML scooters are similar, in most respects, to a Piaggio PX, and will give you a good idea of how things should be. Look at as many as you can, and hear them running; it will help when it comes to checking one out for yourself. Next, start enquiring about scooters for sale. Have a look at the questions below; you might want to ask some of them before committing to a viewing.

Where is the Vespa?
The days of finding lots of two-stroke Vespas for sale in the local paper are long gone, but there should still be a few within a reasonable distance. If you're after a particular model, budget for the extra time and money needed to go and view one.

Cost of getting it home?
If you're buying a roadworthy scooter, you need to arrange insurance. Consider getting a friend to drop you off, so you can ride the scooter home. If you're going for a restoration project, costs will rapidly mount. Van hire, or the pricier option of getting someone to collect it for you, will need to be factored in, so always get quotes for these services first.

Dealer or private sale?
There are plenty of scooter dealers around, and your local motorcycle shop may even have a Vespa tucked away in a corner. Dealers always charge more, as they have overheads to cover (premises, guarantee costs, advertising, staff wages etc). The plus-side of buying from a dealer, is that they have clear, legal responsibilities, so you'll have some redress should anything go wrong.

Reasons for sale?
If the scooter is being sold by a shop, then the reason is obvious; it's the way it makes its living. Private vendors may have a wide range of reasons (most of which will be perfectly legitimate), but ask anyway; the question may take some by surprise, and a hurried response might raise some doubts.

Viewing – where and when?
Always arrange a viewing in daylight, preferably when it isn't raining (a damp sheen can make even the most faded paintwork look half-reasonable). Make sure you view the scooter at the address on the ownership documents. Avoid anyone who only provides a mobile contact number, and insists on bringing the Vespa to you or meeting at a public spot, no matter how convenient that may sound. Arrange to see the scooter on a day when it hasn't been run, as how it starts will be important.

Condition?
Before you go and look, ask the seller for an honest appraisal of the Vespa's

condition. Tell them you're coming some distance, as this can make many people own up to the blatantly obvious or immediately noticeable defects, at least. If the scooter doesn't sound very promising, or the seller is vague, don't waste your time; there are plenty more out there.

All original specification?

Historically, scooter owners have been keen on individualising their rides; the subsequent desirability of which is down to the prospective owner – beauty being very much in the eye of the beholder. Standard specifications, and factory colours, are generally worth the most (and are always easier to sell-on, if you change your mind). Sensible upgrades like the addition of electronic ignition to older models shows the owner was keen to actually use the machine.

Matching data?

Frame and engine numbers are discussed more thoroughly later, but before you view, ask the seller if they are clearly visible, and match the paperwork. If it's in any way dodgy, they'll at least know you'll be checking when you turn up. If you're after a particular model, do your homework first; when you see a scooter in the metal, you'll know whether it has the right trim and fittings for its type and age. This is particularly important if you'll be looking at a scooter imported from the Far East, as they often end up with many non-standard parts.

Is the seller the legal owner?

In the UK, the ownership papers (V5C) record the registered keeper – not necessarily the legal owner. Ask the seller if they are the actual owner; if they're not, get contact details of whoever is, and make sure that they know the vehicle is for sale. Make sure there's no outstanding Hire Purchase, or other loan, secured on the vehicle.

Does the scooter have an MoT?

All countries have some sort of roadworthiness check, which, in the UK, is referred to as an MoT. Check how long it's valid for, and make sure that the frame number matches the document. Don't rely on a current certificate too much; it only reflects the scooter's condition at the time of the test. Road tax is cheap for scooters, and pre-1973 ones are tax-free in the UK (many other countries operate similar schemes). As the new owner, you are responsible for taxing the vehicle before using it on the road. Tax is no longer transferred with the vehicle.

How can you pay?

A pocketful of cash can be a useful lever, when bargaining over the final price. If you're uncomfortable carrying a large sum of cash around with you, ask if you can pay by cheque, and collect the scooter when it has cleared. A Bankers Draft in the current owner's name is another option (although some sellers are wary of these, due to a rise in counterfeits). Dealers are usually the most flexible sellers, allowing the use of credit cards, or arranging finance on the deal.

Are you insured to drive it once you've paid?

Not actually a question for the seller, but still something to bear in mind. Sometimes, your existing cover will extend to riding a scooter, or a friend may be able to ride it on their policy. Whilst cheap, this isn't really recommended, as the level of cover is often the legal minimum.

Professional checks?
It may be possible to have a scooter checked by a motoring organisation, but it wouldn't be a mainstream vehicle for them to deal with. If you feel that professional help is needed, try to find a specialist who can look it over for you; they'll be familiar with the Vespa's idiosyncrasies. Check they have liability insurance, in case they miss anything which might ultimately prove expensive.

Data checks?
There are national organisations which can check if the scooter has been stolen, written off, or has any outstanding hire purchase payments due on it. In the UK, the best known company is HPI www.hpi.co.uk; it usually provides a compensation scheme, should any of the information it supplies later prove to be inaccurate. There are similar organisations in other countries.

– these items will really help

This book

The major defects that you're likely to find in any prospective purchase, are outlined in this book. It can be all too easy to forget important checks in the excitement of viewing your future scooter but if you work your way through the sections methodically, using the unique marking system, it will help make up your mind (and could save you hard-earned cash).

Magnet

A Vespa frame is a steel pressing (like a car) and, unless you're really good at spotting filler, a magnet will help check just how good the metal is. Take a weak magnet (a strong one may grip through

Make sure you have the right gear for a thorough examination.

the filler, defeating the object). Use it with care; don't scrape it across the paint surface. Remember that you're looking at someone else's pride and joy (until you stump up the money to make it yours).

Overalls

At some point, you will need to grovel on the ground (to check under the floors or examine the exhaust). There will also be a fair bit of kneeling involved. Overalls can be removed, so you can test-drive the scooter without parking a muddy bottom on the seat.

Torch

For the Vespas few hidden nooks and crannies, you'll need a torch. A small Maglite, or similar, is big enough.

Spectacles (if you need them for close work)

You'll be taking a close look at the paint for sub-surface problems; if you need glasses for this type of inspection, make sure that you have them with you.

Small screwdriver

Rust inspection is vital, and an electrical screwdriver to probe suspect areas is very useful. Some sellers may be less than impressed if you use it too vigorously, though.

A friend

He, or she, doesn't need to be an expert, but a second pair of eyes can be useful. An extra, unbiased opinion can help to keep your feet on the ground, and debate any issues that you've found. An experienced scooter club member is even better!

Having located a suitable scooter, asked all the necessary questions over the phone, and assembled your inspection equipment, you should now be confronting a classic Vespa in the metal. At this stage, the most important thing is not to let your heart rule your head – so keep calm. Dispel those daydreams about cruising through city streets, the centre of everyone's attention, and bring yourself back down to earth by remembering just how long it took to get the money together to buy this thing. It should be possible to eliminate dodgy, overpriced heaps quite quickly, hence this 15 minute evaluation. By the end of this section, you should know if the scooter is worth spending more time on. Some of these initial areas will be subjected to a far more searching scrutiny during the full inspection, so don't linger too long just yet; for the moment, aim for a good, general overview.

Paperwork

First, ensure the ownership papers are present, matching the registration plate. Check that the person showing you the scooter is the person named on them, and that you're at the stated address. Chassis and engine number checks will be dealt with later, as they're not always immediately accessible. You might as well make sure that you think this Vespa is going to be worth the effort first, as lots wont be and can be dismissed very quickly. If a valid roadworthiness certificate is in force, check that all its details match too.

Well worn but un-messed with; could be an ideal scooter.

General condition

First impressions are important, but don't fall for a shiny coat of paint, or the glitter of chrome accessories. Start, instead, with how the scooter looks generally; is it shabby and neglected, or does it seem well cared for? How does it sit? The back end should be on the ground, with the front wheel slightly elevated; if both are touching, then the stand (or its brackets) are worn or damaged. If the front sits very high, it has

If the nose is too high, the wrong stand is fitted.

the wrong stand fitted – a common fault with Far Eastern restorations. Walk slowly around the scooter, looking for obvious signs of damage, such as dents, scratches and scrapes on the panels. Look at the handlebar grips; are

Old grips, but they haven't been damaged in a slide.

the ends damaged? Are the balls on the clutch and brake levers scraped? This indicates that the scooter has slid down the road on its side. Is the legshield trim obviously newer than everything else? Again, this can quite easily cover up damage. Is there any rust or bubbling paint on the floor boards, or signs of recent touching up?

Move your head around, letting the light hit the paintwork at an angle. Vespas are pretty slab-sided, and poor attempts at repair with filler should be obvious. Any bloom, where spray-cans have been used to touch-up tatty bits, will also be obvious. Is the scooter still in its factory paint? A complete colour change may simply be down to the owner's particular style or preference; but it may have been forced upon them, through deterioration or damage. Watch out for stickers too; they can be very useful in covering up minor problems or stone chips. If the scooter has been restored, how good do the smaller items look? Are there rusty bolts? Pitted alloy on the luggage hook? Split rubbers on the stand feet? Is the seller claiming a low mileage, but the footbrake rubber is worn out? Is anything missing? Dust covers on hub-nuts often are; if so, is there a split-pin in the nut? Look for little clues that add up to give a bigger picture.

Floorboard rot is easy to spot.

Marked side panel; accident damage, or just a supermarket scrape?

A lovely scooter, with all the little details sorted. Is the one you're checking the same?

Make sure the forks are straight.

Walk to the front of the scooter, and check that the front wheel appears upright in relation to the body, and everything looks in line. Do the same at the rear, checking that the back wheel is vertical. Have a look at the front end, from the right-hand side. Imagine a line, starting at the centre of the hub, going through the steering head, and out of the headset; does it all look straight?

The engine and gearbox are in one unit, pretty much hidden behind the side panel. However, enough is visible to check for any major oil leaks, or signs of damage (such as a scraped or bent kickstart). Have a look at the exhaust, and check that the end is clean, and not clogged with clumps of semi-dry, unburnt two-stroke oil deposits. Put your hand close to it and feel for any heat (to see if the engine has been run immediately prior to your arrival). Turn on the petrol, moving the lever-tab to the right-hand side; check that the scooter is in neutral, then slowly depress the kickstart, feeling for compression as you do so. It should be clearly

The fuel tap in the off position. Rotate it 180 degrees to turn on. The black choke knob simply pulls out.

Feel for compression, or loose or tight spots, as you move the kickstart.

noticeable. If not, the piston, rings or cylinder are worn. Allow the kickstart to ratchet back to the top; turn on the ignition, pull out the choke knob fully, and then push the kickstart down in one smooth, firm movement. The engine should fire immediately (or at least try to). If it hasn't started after two or three kicks, then it isn't in top condition. If it takes a lot of pumping up and down on the kickstart, accompanied by frantic throttle twisting, then you might as well walk away now: this indicates a major problem. It may even extend to damage to the compression-pad face on the crankcase, which requires engine replacement. PXs with electric-start should fire-up with the minimum of churning on the button. The engine might sound a little noisy from cold (most air-cooled two-strokes do), but within a couple of minutes, you should be able to push the choke in and let the engine settle down. The idle should be crisp, even, and quiet, without any surging or unusual noises. Push the front of the scooter down (making sure the back wheel is fully off the ground), then select first gear. Did it go in with a loud, shuddering clunk? Did the lever move past its painted position? If so, there's wear, somewhere in the gear selector mechanism and the cush drive or the clutch is dragging badly. Turn the engine back off.

Standing on the right-hand side, place your foot in front of the stand, and roll the scooter onto its wheels. If you are not used to the weight distribution of a Vespa, it will try and tilt towards you, so be prepared for it. Did the whole bike sag under its own weight, as it rolled off the stand, or did it feel taut? Straddle the scooter and push it gently forward, feeling for any sign of sticking brakes. Pull the front brake on hard, as you continue to push, to check that it works, and see how much the suspension dives. Release, then push forward again; are the brakes sticking now? Did the lever return to its correct position, or is it stuck? If the scooter has disc brakes, do you need to pump the lever, before it grips properly? If so, there may be a leak (or at the very least, the system needs bleeding). Try the same process with the back brake (this takes a bit more care with balance). Bounce the front end up and down, then sit up and down on the seat, to check the rear. Neither end should be noisy while you do this.

Is it worth staying for a longer look?
The answer, of course, depends on the amount of money being asked for the scooter, and the level of expectation attached to that price. If you're looking for a restoration project, then none of the defects you may have uncovered might trouble you. However, unless you're confident with a MIG welder (or have fully budgeted for parts and labour costs), it's still best to avoid anything with extensive frame rot or panel damage. If the scooter is being sold at roughly the going rate, for one in good condition, and you have found rust or faded paint, then it might not warrant wasting any more time. If things seem OK up until now (or at least not so bad that you have definitely been put off), then it's time for a more searching and critical examination. So, get out the overalls; there's some grovelling around in the dirt to be done.

Frame rust is a killer of classic Vespas, as repairs are time consuming and expensive. Unfortunately, corrosion tends to start unseen, getting a grip before it becomes noticeable. If you're going to restore a rusty Vespa, there's only one sure way to get rid of rot; get the frame dipped, cut away affected areas, weld new metal in place, then inject rust-proofer into the body cavity.

A smoky, noisy engine probably needs a complete overhaul or replacement, and neither are cheap. If there's been an engine problem (like broken piston rings), the compression pad may be damaged, and replacement is the only option. It's best to budget for a complete new unit, though if you can rebuild the old one, it will be a nice financial bonus.

Gearbox noises, or problems such as jumping out of gear, also require a complete engine strip. Problems other than noise could be simple (a worn selector box pin housing, worn detents, or simple cable adjustment), but it's your hard earned cash; do you want to take the gamble?

Don't be seduced by good looks; make sure the scooter is genuine. Always check stamped frame numbers against the paperwork. If it's an imported, unregistered scooter, do your homework. Look up model codes, and make sure it matches what you're actually looking at. Many agencies awarding dating certificates now require photos; any problems, and you wont be able to register the scooter.

Scratches, scrapes and minor dents are a real problem. Can you live with them? If not, then are you able to repaint only the affected panels, or will the whole lot need re-doing? Professional paintwork is extremely expensive, so even minor imperfections can add-up to big money. Does the selling price reflect your assessment of the scooter's cosmetic state? If not, move on.

9 Serious evaluation
– 60 minutes for years of enjoyment

Score each section using the boxes as follows:
4 = excellent; 3 = good; 2 = average; 1 = poor. The totting up procedure is detailed at the end of the chapter. Be realistic in your marking!

Spotting defects

It's now time to closely examine the scooter for signs of repair, or bodging used to disguise its true condition. Look through the paint surface for sub-surface scratching or tiny holes (which indicate the presence of filler). Repairers usually try to hide any work at panel edges, so be particularly critical there; it's the best place to find traces of work done. If you're suspicious, compare one side of the scooter to the other; do the curves match? Do the panels fit the same? Try gently running your hands over the surface; it's surprising how sensitive they can be at picking up imperfections. If you're still unsure, use the magnet, and see if it sticks to the surface.

Now is the time to look through the paint surface to spot problems.

A spray-can touch-up has been faded-out around the badge.

Paintwork

If the scooter has had a quick paint blow-over, there will be signs. Look for overspray around the speedo housing,

Check recently painted scooters particularly carefully.

for instance, or on the side of the floor runners. Are the gear numbers and dot on the headset still in a contrasting colour, or have they been sprayed over? New paint isn't necessarily bad, but if there are signs the job was rushed, then that shiny, new surface will not last long before problems start bursting through again. Duff paintwork can be a budget buster; resprays aren't cheap.

Main frame

All Vespa frames are monocoques, made from pressed steel sections spot-welded together (motorcycles, and Vespa's main competitor, the Lambretta, rely on a separate frame). Immensely strong, its big problem is corrosion, with any affected

part weakening the whole structure. The first place to check is under the floor, where there are reinforcing box-sections. The number of these decreased over the years in order to save weight. These box-sections must be in good condition. Give them a good prod, and look for rust – particularly where they're spot-welded to the floor. In bad cases, the corrosion will have spread out into the floor itself, possibly with holing. Check, too, the extreme-rear of the underside, where the engine unit is mounted, as mud and other road-muck can accumulate (with obvious results). Whilst there, check the edges of the pan where the trim is mounted. If the scooter has fallen over, or slid down the road on

Check the underside of floor and box sections for rust.

its side, new trim may have been used to cover-up scrapes and minor imperfections. Be dubious of any scooter with a thick layer of freshly applied underseal: it may be covering up something nasty.

Time to get back off your knees, and check the top surface of the floorboards. Lift any rubber mats that might be fitted, and check for rust blisters. These can sprout just about anywhere, but pay particular attention to the joint with the central tunnel (it is the most likely starting point). Also, check the area around the centre-stand mounting bolts; rotten frames can badly distort the seams here. Further back, there should be a series of clearly visible spot-welds, where the rear section meets the centre tunnel. This, again, suffers from swelling and blistering, and

Rot often starts at the back, just in front of the swinging arm.

Floor edges rust, and are hidden by the trim.

The whole of the floor boards need checking ...

... as does the seam, to the rear body side.

The area around the rear panel securing pin rusts.

Check the area behind the front wheel for rot and accident damage.

the top layer can split. If the side panel has a locking pin here, expect rust blistering around it. Check the front of the legshields (directly behind the front wheel) for corrosion from rot spreading from the box-section, behind.

Above the rear panels, look for signs of bubbling or blistering paint, indicating rust working its way out from the inside (or poorly applied filler trying to disguise that fact). The

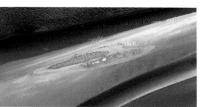

Frame cavities can rust from the inside; look for signs above the side panels.

spot-welded seam from the seat, running to the rear, and the surrounding metal are also prone to rust. Check the area around the rear number plate. The seller probably wont want you to unscrew it to have a look, but corrosion can usually be seen creeping out. If the back end is very rusty, it can often result in stress-cracking. On PXs, rust can also start where the small,

The seam, down from the seat to the back light, corrodes, as does the surrounding metal.

Check all around the rear number plate for bubbling corrosion.

plastic rear-bumper is attached; on Mark 1 T5s, it can start where the front chin-spoiler is mounted to the floor boards. There are more rust areas to check, but they'll be addressed once the side panels have been removed.

The other concern with the frame is twisting, or other damage caused in an accident. If it's been subjected to a front impact, there may be a crease in the curved area, under the horn-cast, or even in the central tunnel. If it was heavy enough, a rear impact will have caused creasing, too, so check the rear sweeps of the frame carefully.

If you find extensive rusting or damage, now is the time to walk away – unless you are looking at a very rare scooter.

Make sure the side panels are securely mounted.

Side panels

There are a variety of attachment methods for these panels. Unless you are familiar with them, it's better to allow the owner to remove and replace them for you. Before you do, double-check they're mounted securely, and not loose. If an older model has a toolbox in the left-hand panel, it generally means that it's not quickly detachable; it's held by screws, accessed from inside the cowling. Cooling louvres are easily damaged – and very hard to repair – so make sure that they're straight. Once the side panels are off, examine the rear of the frame for rust and accident

damage. The spare wheel, on the left-hand side, may obstruct your view, but you should still be able to get a good idea of the general condition. Leave the panels off, for the moment, as you continue your examination. Small frame Vespas don't have removable panels, like the larger models, only a small engine access door.

Small frames have a removable engine cover.

Numbers

Now is the best time to check that the frame number matches the Vehicle Registration Document, and the area around the number hasn't been tampered with. Look for signs of re-stamping, or a new section of frame welded in place. In some markets, models came with a riveted plate, containing all the scooter details. These are usually mounted under the

petrol tap, or on the side of the central tunnel. Some have a small, single plate, containing only the chassis number,

Some versions have external plates, like this German GS. Don't rely on them alone, check the frame itself.

Frame numbers should be clear and untampered with. This one has been rubbed down for identification, then primed.

riveted near the stamped number. Don't rely on these plates alone; check them against the factory number, stamped in the frame. If you're buying an unregistered import, make sure that the number matches the model that's being sold (Vespa frame codes are freely available on the internet). Frame and engine numbers are generally located as follows:

Small frame
With the engine cover hinged down, the frame number should be visible on the frame; it's at the top of the recess that the cover sits in. The engine number can be found below the rear shock mount, adjacent to the gearbox filer-plug.

P Series, Sprint, Rally
The frame number is located behind the right-hand panel, towards the back of the frame. The

Engine numbers are cast into the alloy of the swinging arm.

engine number is stamped into a flat area of the swinging arm, visible behind the exhaust.

VBB type
The frame number can be found stamped in the body, behind the left side-panel (which is usually fixed, so use the torch you brought with you). Engine number is in the same location as P series, above.

Vespa engines are built from matched halves, so check that the two sides have the same casting code, engraved at the back. You may need to wipe away some muck and oil to see them.

Headset

Make sure there's no movement relative to the forks, and there's no lift when you pull-up on the bars. The alloy can be damaged from a fall, so look for cracks or signs of repair. PXs have plastic tops, which are easy to scratch, and tend to fade.

Check the headset for cracking or other damage.

Mudguard

The front mudguard is extremely rot prone. It loses paint at the edges, allowing surface rust to form. The spot-welded seam is an open invitation for road water and debris to penetrate between the two sections, causing the joint to swell and split with rust. This is both unsightly, and almost impossible to stop, once it has a hold. Finally, the mudguard mount to the forks suffers in exactly the same way; look at the area under the horn-cast carefully for damage or blistering. T5s have a seam-free guard; an improvement over other models.

Mudguards rust at the seam, and under the horn-cast.

If the forks turn too far, the lock stops are damaged.

Forks

With the front end off the ground, lightly hold the grips with your finger tips. Slowly move the bars, from lock to lock, feeling for any roughness or tight spots. The bars should contact the lock-stops at the same point on each side, and nothing should touch the legshields. If the stops are damaged, there may be telltale notches on the trim (at the top of the shields), where the headlight rim has caught. The handlebar grips should be secure and undamaged. Move to the front of the scooter, grasp the fork leg, and try and push and pull it towards

Give the forks a good yank to check the head bearings.

you. It's better to get someone to hold the back of the scooter whilst you do this, so you can use greater force. If you feel movement in the fork stem, the steering head bearings are shot; cheap, but labour intensive to replace.

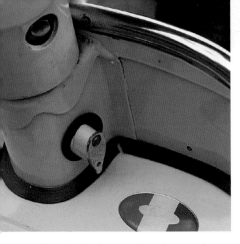

Steering locks are often damaged, or missing their keys.

Later ignition locks should be checked for signs of attempted theft.

Steering lock/ignition switch

Examine this carefully, as it may have been forced in the past. Make sure that the key operates with precision, or the lock maybe damaged. Missing keys for separate steering locks are common, but replacing a steering lock can be expensive, as older models may require fork disassembly.

Brakes

Discs shouldn't be scored, have a noticeable wear lip at the outer edge, or have cracks around the holes. Pads should be just visible through the caliper opening. Pads are cheap to replace, but make sure the pad-pin isn't rusty or heavily burred

Discs shouldn't be ridged or cracked.

The fluid in the reservoir should be clean, with no signs of leaking.

at the end. Check the bleed nipple (they go rusty and snap off). The hydraulic line, and all joints, should be clean, dry, and securely attached, where clipped to the mudguard. The fluid in the reservoir should be a clear, golden yellow, with no leaks or staining in the area. Check drums (for bodges), and cable attachments. A lever at an angle greater than 90 degrees to the cable indicates worn linings.

On adjusters like this, gauge wear by the amount of thread visible, or by lever angle, on the earlier types.

Suspension [4] [3] [2] [1]

Depending on model, the front suspension will either have a separate spring-and-damper, or a combined unit, in a sleeve. Either way, give each a good pull about, to make sure that they are secure. Also have a look at the bottom bushes, for signs of splitting or shrinkage. Oil leaks from any damper (shock absorber) are unacceptable. Take the scooter off its stand, hold the front brake on, tight, and push the front end up and down; feel how much damping there is. Do the same check at the back end. Everything should be pretty much silent whilst you bounce, with perhaps a quiet squish, as the oil in the dampers is displaced. If there is any squeaking, or clunking, there's play somewhere,

Shock absorber mounts should be secure, without any play.

so double-check the mountings. If the shocks include metal covers, make sure that they have not corroded through at the back. Adjustable shock absorbers are a common upgrade and improve the suspension.

The same checks are necessary on earlier, separate spring front suspension, too.

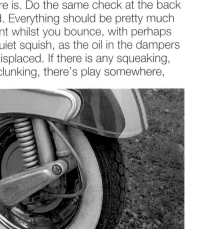

Engine

The Vespa motor is extremely well designed and built, developed over several decades to provide reliable service for many years. Problems usually stem from general deterioration with age, and/or lack of care by previous owners. Well maintained, and left in standard form, they're capable of racking up enormous mileages, for a small two-stroke.

Start by having a good look for leaks. The crankcases are split vertically, and if they have been apart before, the mating surfaces may be damaged. Look for gasket-goo oozing from the joint: it shouldn't need it. The outside of the cases gather muck (often oily) from the cylinder-base leaking, which should be fairly obvious. Staining further up is likely to be from a leaking carb; needle-valve

You should know what a healthy engine sounds like before starting your search; how does yours compare?

Look for fuel leaks on upper casings.

Check for leaks at the barrel-to-case joint, and at the exhaust downpipe clamp.

On disc brake PXs a leaking hub seal means an engine strip to replace it, so check carefully.

tips wear, allowing flooding. On small frames, the carb is inside the frame, under the seat, so you'll have to check that later. The gear selector box area should be free from leaks. Whilst you're checking, have a look at the rear of the brake backplate; the gearbox output shaft seals perish, letting oil seep out around the mount (and, in very bad cases, out of the bottom edge). The kickstart shaft oil-seal weeps, too.

Ask the owner if you can remove the gearbox level plug (use a large, flat bladed screwdriver), which will tell you two things; whether the oil level is correct, and by smelling some of the oil, whether there's any petrol contamination (a sign of crank-seal wear, requiring a full strip to fix). On small frames, crank-seal problems lead to the gearbox oil level dropping, as oil is dragged into the engine, and burnt. This shows as a large, unusually aromatic cloud, when the motor is running.

Remove the level plug, if allowed; it can tell you a lot.

Grab hold of the flywheel, and try to push and pull it, in and out. A tiny amount of movement is acceptable, but anything more, and the main bearings are worn, causing the crank to float. Try rocking the flywheel diagonally to confirm this. On vory worn engines, the flywheel may even rub against the cover, so look for signs of that happening.

Give the flywheel a good wiggle.

You'll already know the engine starts (from the 15 minute examination), but it now needs further checking. Start it again, listening to the idle more carefully. It should sound crisp, with a clear, sharp, two-stroke pop: if it sounds lethargic, and smokes a lot, then the engine and exhaust probably need a de-coke. If there's a rhythmic slapping sound (it may not be very loud), then the piston and/or bore are worn. This is usually accompanied by an excess of blue smoke, from the exhaust. A rebore will fix this, but if you're looking at a T5, a complete new barrel and piston will be needed; they're Nikasil lined, with a hardened surface that exchanges a – theoretically – longer life, against the ability to rebore. A light, tinkling noise will usually indicate small-end wear, whilst a harder-edged knock means that the big-end bearing is suffering. A constant, heavy rumble is usually a main bearing problem. If you hear a light, chattering sound, try pulling the clutch in; if the noise stops, then the basket (clutch bell) is worn, and the plates are rattling in grooves that they've cut into its sides. This should also show up as a heavy pull on the lever.

Now, rev the engine gently; piston slap will decrease with revs, and big-end, and mains problems, should only get louder. The engine should gain revs cleanly, and not stumble, or hesitate (which usually means there's a carb problem). At higher revs, let go of the throttle quickly; you may get a solitary clunk, which indicates early stages of big-end wear. The throttle should shut immediately, under its own return-spring pressure (but they sometimes stick). If there's a popping sound as the engine drops back to idle, there's an air leak, or hole in the exhaust. As the engine warms, it should get smoother, and smoke less than when cold. If, instead, it gets rougher and noisier, then it's getting tired. Leave it idling, and move the bars to their extremes, left and right (making sure the engine doesn't rev-up while you do so), then rev it gently at each full-lock, to make sure that the throttle cable isn't sticking. Turn off the engine. If it tries to run-on, then the timing may be out, it may be running weak, or, if it is a small frame, the crank oil-seals might be shot.

Exhaust

Standard Vespa exhausts are discrete, restrictive, and rot prone. The down-pipe corrodes, and there are often leaks where they meet the barrel stub. The baffles rot away inside, leading to rattles and vibration. They also bung-up with unburnt two-stroke oil (less of a problem if the owner has used a low-ash, semi-synthetic oil). The Sito Plus range – a common replacement – offers a small increase in power, but with a slightly higher noise output. Expansion chambers are often fitted, but their desirability depends on the state-of-tune, in other parts of the engine and carburettor. If they've simply been slapped on, then power, economy, and reliability could well

Standard exhausts are restrictive and rust-prone.

be impaired. If a spare wheel is important to you, make sure aftermarket chambers allow easy rear wheel removal, whilst still in place; on large frames, ensure a spare wheel can still be carried. If the scooter was first used after January 1985 (in the UK), check non-standard exhausts for the BSAU 193 stamp.

Expansion chambers; popular, but how would you change the rear wheel, here?

Engine mounts ④ ③ ② ①

At the front, the Vespa engine is held in the frame by a long bolt. The bolt passes through a cast-alloy swinging arm, integral with one of the crankcase-halves. Inside the casting are rubber isolating sleeves, bonded to a hollow steel tube. These sleeves can wear, allowing the engine to tilt away from the perpendicular. Check this by looking for uneven tread wear, on one side of the tyre, and by looking at wheel inclination, from the rear. The second problem, in this area, is that the pin can seize in the inner-arm sleeve, allowing the whole lot to pivot with suspension movement.

Make sure the arm pin hasn't seized.

This eventually causes the mounting eyes in the frame to wear oval, so watch the bolt-head closely, while someone pushes the back end up and down. The back of the engine is held in place by the shock absorber, which bolts directly to the casing. Have a look to ensure that the rubber bushes are not split or missing. On scooters that have seen very hard, use the casing may even be cracked. The top end is attached to the frame by another rubber mount, hidden out of view. Get someone to hold the front end of the scooter down, whilst it is on the stand, to lift the rear clear of the ground. Then, firmly grasp the shocker, and give it a good tug about; look and feel for movement, at the top.

The rear shock absorber attaches the back of the engine to the frame.

Tuning

Initially, a tuned scooter may have a lot of appeal, but the reality may not live up to expectations. If a tuning kit has been professionally fitted, the crankcases re-cut to match, a suitable complimentary expansion chamber added, clutch beefed-up, timing reset, and the fuel system adjusted or replaced, then the result may be excellent. The seller should have receipts for all this, as it would have been a sizeable outlay. A DIY tune-up – with no regard to the new flow characteristics of a big-bore cylinder, or its ignition requirements – is a recipe for seizure, and holed pistons. It's also perfectly possible that, even if the engine manages to keep going, nothing has been added to performance, and, in all probability, fuel economy and reliability will have suffered. Vespa took great care to ensure their engines would provide many years of service; make sure that any changes are actually an improvement. The following are some of the kits that are commonly found.

Large frame

PX125/150 models (also two-port Sprint).

The DR 180 (sometimes sold under the Olympia name), which offers little in absolute performance gain, but increases useable torque. The Malossi 166cc, which offers a good power-boost, but with 'peakier' delivery. Polini sells a 177cc kit, which falls between these two, and is often chosen for touring applications. Finally, there is the Pinasco 177cc setup, which is more expensive, and rarer.

PX200 (also Rally 180/200)

The Malossi 210 is the most popular, being both reliable and potent. Once again, Polini and Pinasco both make their own kits for this engine, but both are less common.

T5

This model has not been abandoned by aftermarket tuning firms; a 152cc Polini kit, and a 172cc Malossi kit are readily available. The highly rated Pinasco 162cc has been discontinued; if you find a scooter with one, finding a replacement piston could be troublesome.

Small frame

The small frame Vespa has been a favourite with racers all over Europe since its introduction. Even now, the market for bolt-on bits is both innovative, and flourishing. You're most likely to find ones by Malossi, who make four, good quality kits, from 75cc to 135cc. All offer a good performance boost, but make the engine reliant on revs to produce that power. Polini are also a quality option, with six kits, from 50cc to 130cc, all offering more power, with slightly torquier output. Finally, DR, which come in four sizes from 75cc to 130cc, offers a good, torquey output, but has a lower, outright performance. There are other kits around, by the likes of Falc, Quattrini, and Parmakit, but these are much less common.

To make the most of a tuned engine's capabilities, the gearing should be up-rated too. Otherwise, you end up with acceleration like a ballistic missile, but little gain in top speed. Ironically though, on a 200, top gear may be dropped, reducing the gap with third, to enable the engine to rev-out. Ask if any gearing changes have been made; without them, a tuned scooter can be a buzzy, frustrating ride over longer distances. Unfortunately, the possible problems don't end there. You can end up with a very fast scooter, but be unable to use it at maximum speed (except in very short bursts) as the cooling which is fine in standard trim can quickly become marginal, with a hard running, big-bore kit under the cowl.

Make sure the fuel tank isn't rusty inside.

Fuel system

With the seat raised, remove the fuel filler cap, and shine your torch inside. The fuel should be a light, almost clear, yellowy colour (colours change with premix models depending on oil make). You should be able to see the clean metal of the tank-inner through it. Look for rust – especially if the scooter has been sitting for a long time. Getting rid of rust is time consuming and expensive; it could be cheaper to buy a new tank (if they are available for that model). If the fuel is darker, it's old; change it before using the scooter regularly. If the scooter has autolube, check the level, and if the system has been disconnected for any reason, ask why, and ensure the carburettor has been re-jetted, to compensate. On small frames, there should be a small luggage compartment, in front of the tank. Take it out and you will see the carburettor; have a look for leaks, or staining.

Caps often leak, staining the side panels

Wheels and tyres

Wheels can be 8, 9 or (far more commonly) 10 inch. 9 inch versions, fitted to early, small frames, are rare, and getting new tyres can be a frustrating business. Options for 8 inch are not too bad, and 10 inch are well catered for, in a variety of compounds, from touring to race. Wear-rates can be high, so check how much tread is left, and budget accordingly. Check the sidewalls for damage, from kerbing or running under-inflated. If the scooter hasn't been used for three years or more, budget to replace the tyres as a matter of course. Wheels are split-rim (apart from the very recent arrival of aftermarket, tubeless variants). Check them for rust, and ensure the halves are securely bolted together. Split-washers, or self-locking nuts, should be clearly visible. There are two types of hub

Check for tread wear, especially at the rear.

mounting; the four-bolt type (which sit towards the middle of the wheel), and the star-type (which has the mounting studs on small, cast projections on the edge), with four or five mounts, depending on type. Make sure that the studs are all present, on the latter style; they can snap-off if treated carelessly (ensure none have been replaced with nuts and bolts).

The early, four-bolt hub ...

... and later five-point.

Wheel bearings

While you're examining the wheels, you may as well check the bearings. Grab each rim in turn, and gently push and pull. There should be no play at the front, and just the smallest amount at the rear (due to the design of the drive you are actually checking the output shaft bearing) – but it should be very slight. Try turning the front wheel, very slowly, with a finger tip; it's often possible to feel roughness, indicating wear. Spin the wheel, too, and listen – although, if a bearing is so worn that you can hear it, you should have picked up the wear by wobbling. Shake the rim with more vigour, to try and detect play in the fork pivot; if you find any, it's expensive to rectify.

Check front wheel bearings by giving the wheel a good pull.
P series scooters always seem to have a little play in the front hub.

Lights

First, make sure they all work. This may take a little fiddling with the unmarked switch gear. Blown bulbs may simply be that, or it could indicate that the charging system is not functioning properly. On models without a battery, the engine must be running to get lights. Expect them to be dim at idle, but they should brighten, as revs increase.

Switchgear may have no markings, and take a little figuring out.

Check the reflector for rust, or silver flaking off.

They shouldn't flicker, once brightened, or there is a continuity or voltage regulator problem. Check the headlight reflector for corrosion, discolouration, or flaking silvering (all of which will be a future roadworthiness test fail). The brake light should work off the foot pedal, regardless of model, and any sold new in the UK, after April 1986, should have a switch on the front handlebar lever, too.

Indicators   4️⃣ 3️⃣ 2️⃣ 1️⃣

On P series scooters, indicators are meant to flash out of sequence, front-to-rear (not together, as is the norm). They're prone to earthing problems, and often malfunction. Some markets (such as the USA) had indicators fitted to earlier 6-volt models; these are even more troublesome, and were often removed, making them a rare fitment today. Indicator switches should be positive in action, and there should be a working warning light in the instrument panel. All lenses should be undamaged, and not faded.

Indicators are unreliable, especially 6-volt versions.

Trim   4️⃣ 3️⃣ 2️⃣ 1️⃣

Most scooters left the factory with very little in the way of brightwork. Earlier scooters used alloy, in the main, for any fittings, which should be examined for discolouration and pitting. Later versions relied heavily on plastic, which loses its colour and becomes brittle with age. For rarer models, finding the right trim can be difficult, so do your homework beforehand and check that it's all present and correct. There's a lot of remanufactured trim on the market, which varies in quality, and adherence to the original design.

Early alloy badging is fragile, and modern copies vary in quality.

Later plastic badges tend to fade.

Seat

The most common seat problem is split vinyl. On older models, the foam loses its shape, leaving a saggy cover. Metal-frame seats can suffer from rust, and snapped springs. Recovering is not too arduous, and even complete replacement seats are reasonably priced. Most original styles are being remanufactured, along with a plethora of sportier, or comfier, options. Make sure that the seat is securely mounted (give it a good wiggle), the hinge is not seizing up, and that the lock (where fitted) works properly. Replacing a lock is straightforward and inexpensive, but add it to the haggle list. Whilst the seat is up, check for leaking fuel around the cap, and that the wiring for the level-sender (where fitted) is in place. Check that there Is no rust, breaking-out, under there, too.

Seat covers easily split.

Seat locks are cheap and easy to replace.

Instruments

These vary from the non-existent (like some Italian market 50s, lacking even a speedo), up to the T5 Mark 1, with its fuel-gauge, rev-counter, and array of warning lights. The only advice, here, is to make sure that if it is fitted, it works. Speedo-drives can be short lived, so check the accumulated mileage against that on the last test certificate. If it hasn't risen, it might just be a faulty odometer; but assume it's the whole speedo head or drive, in the hub, until a test drive can confirm the cause. Genuine replacements are no problem for later scooters, but copies for earlier models vary tremendously (some don't work straight out of the box). If the speedo is a really rare model, there are specialist restorers who can resuscitate just about anything – but it is expensive.

Until the early '80s, instruments were very basic.

Mark 1 T5s were better equipped, but the circuit boards on these panels frequently fail, so check carefully.

Electrical system

Vespa electrics were built to a price. After all, Vespas were originally designed as short-hop commuters, and age will have done little to improve their performance. On 6-volt points-equipped scooters, the rotor's magnetism may well be weak. This can contribute to a range of problems, including poor starting, or cutting out at low revs, with the lights on. Straightforward and inexpensive, re-magnetisation was once common, but there aren't many place able to do this, now. If a battery is fitted, check for signs of overcharging, like acid staining, or stripped paint, and rusty panels in the immediate vicinity. A healthy battery will show around 13 volts, and once the engine is running, this should rise with revs. If it exceeds 14.5 (or doesn't budge at all), the regulator is most likely at fault. All batteries should be properly secured with a rubber strap; terminal connections should be tight, with the positive one covered. Electric start-motors fail, and often the battery is blamed; replacement starters are expensive, and awkward to fit. Look for signs of DIY tampering, with odd colour wires, or plastic 'choc-block' connectors. Be suspicious of plastic-sleeved crimp connectors too (there are some terrible versions on sale at autojumbles and on the net).

The electrical system; basic, but reasonably reliable.

Test ride

Some sellers are reluctant to allow a complete stranger to ride-off on their scooter, and with good reason; theft is far from uncommon. To ease their concerns, take along your driving licence and proof of insurance. If your insurance only covers you third-party, then it'll have to be a case of "I bend it, I mend it". You can also leave the vehicle you arrive in/on, as security (assuming that it's of equal value). Dealers should be more amenable to a test drive than private sellers, but they'll still require adequate evidence of identity.

Once you've passed that hurdle, try to ride the scooter for at least 10 minutes, on as wide-a-range of roads as possible. If you're unsure of how the scooter should be (and have no past experience to compare with), your judgements can only be general. The scooter should accelerate promptly and smoothly, and anything 125cc and above should feel quite nippy in the lower gears. If it feels hesitant, then clears, suspect a carb problem. Any misfiring is likely to be ignition related. If it just feels slow, all the time, then general engine wear may be the cause. Gears should engage cleanly. Getting used to twist-grip selection can take time, and missed gears are a possibility for the inexperienced. If you find that you're missing them more often than you should (even when taking extra care), then there may be a problem with cable adjustment (or the selector box pin, or detent is worn). If the scooter drops out of gear on acceleration, particularly in second and third, then the cruciform selector mechanism is worn. This requires a complete engine strip-down to sort out. If all the gears clonk as they go in, then the cush drive is worn. Once again, this requires a major strip to rectify. If any one gear is noisy, the teeth may be chipped (often a result of untreated, cruciform wear). Due to the type of direct-drive chosen by Piaggio, the gearbox bearings have a hard life. Listen for a constant droning, often most easily heard on the over-run. Wheel bearing noise, on the other hand, fluctuates, with a distinctive 'wow wow' noise, which increases with road speed.

The clutch shouldn't slip under load, or after a gear change. Sitting in first gear, with the lever pulled in, the scooter shouldn't try to creep forward, or the clutch is dragging. On pre-P series, disc equipped scooters, the clutch can be sharp on uptake, causing a lurch (until you get used to it).

Having spent time listening for potential engine and box defects, concentrate next on the handling. This should be stable and safe. Any tendency to head for one side of the road, or the other (excluding any heavy camber on the surface), probably indicates that the frame is misaligned. A general vagueness of direction is more likely to be shot steering head and bearings. Worn shock absorber mounts, and fork links, can produce this, too, so listen for clonks, over bumps. The suspension is likely to feel a little bouncy, but shouldn't lurch uncontrollably after hitting road imperfections. If the back end feels vague, and insecure, when cornering, then the engine and rear shock rubber-mounts are likely to be worn.

Find a straight, quiet stretch of road, and – once you're sure it's safe for you and other road users to do so – try the brakes. Compared to more modern

On the test ride, ensure the rear brake works correctly – but it can be insensitive, so take care not to lock it up.

A Rally 200 or PX200; all models have the same basic problems. How did yours fare?

scooters, front drum brakes are relatively weak, and need a good pull. Discs are fine, and should feel powerful. If there's a pulsing, back through the lever, then the disc is warped, or the drum oval. In very bad cases, you may feel the forks bobbing up and down. The back brake can be insensitive, so until you get used to it, take care not to lock it up. It should pull strongly and cleanly; snatching or locking probably indicate oil contamination, from a leaking hub seal. If there's been a bad leak for some time, the brake will be almost completely ineffectual.

Re-check the operation of all lights, indicators, cables etc., whilst on the move, and make sure both speedometer and odometer are working. Return to the seller, and leave the scooter idling, whilst you decide whether this Vespa is worth making an offer on.

Evaluation procedure
Add up the points scored
Score: 100 = Concours; 75+ = good to very good; 50+ = average to good; 25 to 49 = poor to average. Less than 25 = basket case

Scooters scoring over 70 should be useable immediately, and require little in the way of repair (but will need continuing maintenance whilst in use). Scooters scoring between 25 and 49 need a full restoration, the cost of which will be pretty much the same, regardless of score. Those scoring between 50 and 74 need to be assessed, so the purchase price reflects accurately the amount of work required.

10 Auctions
– sold! Another way to buy your dream

Mainstream Vespa models are not common at classic vehicle auctions. However, rarer variants are turning up more frequently in catalogues, as their value continues to rise, so it's worth a moment to consider this alternative route to your dream purchase.

Pros and cons

Pros: Bargains can be found, with prices often lower than a dealer, and even private sales, depending on demand on the day. Another bonus is that the auction house will usually have checked all the legalities of ownership before the sale, and any supporting paperwork is open to view.

Cons: You'll have little time to inspect the scooter, and (almost certainly) won't be able to give it a test ride. Many vehicles end up at auction because they need some work; it's up to you to decide how much work, and its probable cost. It's also possible to get caught up in the excitement of bidding, and end up paying more than you wanted. Set yourself a figure, and stick to it.

Which auction?

Scooter magazines may list upcoming auctions of interest, as does the classic car press (vehicles are often combined in one sale). Auctioneers usually have websites, with pictures of vehicles and dates of upcoming events that they're in. Past sales results are often listed too, which can give an idea of the current state of the market.

Catalogue and payment details

Buying the catalogue gives you a list of the vehicles in the auction. It also acts as your entry ticket to viewing days, and the big event itself. Machine details will usually be on the skimpy side, but should include basics, such as; number of owners, service history, mileage (if verifiable), plus a guide price that the auction house thinks it should make. The catalogue should also include the terms and conditions of the sale, how to pay, and the amount of buyer's premium and VAT to be added to the hammer price. If you win, a deposit is usually required immediately, and any outstanding amount settled within 24 hours.

Buyer's premium

A buyer's premium may be added to the final price; remember to factor this into your budget. It's not unusual for further, local taxes to be added, too, depending on the state or country.

Viewing

In some instances, it's possible to view well before the auction, and on the day of the sale itself. Staff from the auction house should be available to answer any queries you may have. Ask to hear the scooter running, and look at any paperwork they have. Take every opportunity to examine the machine closely, before bidding.

Bidding

Auctions are exciting, and it's all too easy to be swept along by the euphoria of it all.

Set the maximum amount that you're willing to bid firmly in your head, and stick to it. If you're new to auctions, get there early, and watch earlier lots go through, to see how other people bid. When your particular scooter comes up, bid early, and make sure the auctioneer has you firmly in their sight; that way, they'll keep coming back to you for your reaction to other peoples' bids.

If you lack any further interest in a lot, make sure you show this by shaking your head in an exaggerated manner. If, on the other hand, you win, you'll have to show your Registered Bidder number. If the scooter didn't reach its reserve, go to the office anyway, as the auctioneers may contact the owner if your bid was close, and they think it's a fair amount.

Successful bid

With the scooter won, the next issue is getting it home. If you're unable to drive it, due to condition or insurance, for example, then the auctioneers should have a list of suitable companies who will do it for you, for a fee. If the scooter is legal, then there may be short-term insurance available at the sale, to ride it home (although a phone call to your usual broker will usually yield something cheaper). Never be tempted to ride away from an auction without all the legal necessities in place, as the Police often wait near sales, to catch those foolish enough to try.

Internet auctions

There are undoubtedly some bargains to be had via the internet, but sadly they're very much in the minority. Never buy anything without seeing it in the metal first (unless it's so cheap that it's worth more as spares than the amount you'll pay). Don't be tempted by something hundreds of miles away, without thinking about the time and money needed to get it home. Just like a real auction, it's easy to get carried away, so set a final figure, and don't be tempted to go over it.

There have been cases of outright fraud on the net, as well as examples of clear misrepresentation, so beware. It's very hard getting your money back if it all goes wrong. Be careful with unregistered restorations, as many come from the Far East (despite what the seller may say), and any subsequent problems with build quality, and getting it legal, will become yours.

Auctioneers

Bonhams	www.bonhams.com
Cheffins	www.cheffins.co.uk
H&H	www.classic-auctions.co.uk
Palmer Snell	www.palmersnell.co.uk
Shannons	www.shannons.com.au
eBay	www.ebay.co.uk or www.ebay.com

11 Paperwork
– correct documentation is essential!

The paper trail
With two-stroke Vespas mostly in the classic arena now, the amount of paperwork that goes with any particular scooter is of increasing importance; whether as provenance, or simply a record of restoration or repair. If work has been carried out by recognised specialists (or main dealers, if a more recent vehicle), then their receipts will add value, or at the very least, make any future sale more attractive.

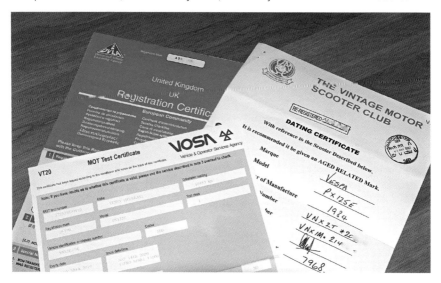

Is all the paperwork present?

Roadworthiness certificate
Virtually every country has a system to check the roadworthiness of vehicles, usually performed annually. Unless you're buying for a restoration project, a valid (preferably long) certificate is pretty much essential. Many owners keep old, expired MoT paperwork, which is very sensible; it provides extra history, plus an independent record of accumulated mileage.

Road fund licence
As mentioned previously, in the UK Road Tax is no longer transferable, and the new owner is responsible for taxing the scooter before using it on public roads. This can be done online by visiting www.gov.uk/tax-disc and using the 12-digit number which is found on the new keeper supplement (V5c/2).

    The scooter will have to be insured first. All records are now stored online and no tax disc is issued, so make sure to keep copies of all on line transactions/reference numbers.

Registration document
In the UK, it's a V5C, in the USA, a Pink Slip, and in France, the Carte Grise; whatever its name, make sure the chassis number on the document matches the one on scooter. Fake ID papers do exist, so have a look on your country's registration website; there's normally advice on how to verify legitimacy. If the engine number is listed, check it too. Engine numbers used to be less important, as swaps were not uncommon, but recent legislation on emissions, and road tax related capacity bands, have resulted in a tightening up in this area.

Dating certificate
If the vehicle is an import (other than through the normal dealer chain), then proof of the date of manufacture may be required in order to register it. This paperwork is usually supplied by a relevant, certified club, or individuals, and will incur a small fee to secure. Do your homework first though; check your proposed purchase can be properly traced. The records for some early Spanish-made Motovespas, for example, are missing, which could prove a problem when you need a certificate.

Service history
Service records, from main or specialist dealers, definitely increase value. Many Vespas are maintained by enthusiastic owners, which need not be a problem (they may even have had better care as a result). A conversation with the seller is usually enough to gauge just how competent they are, and they should have receipts for any parts. Little things may give the game away; using cheap, supermarket, two-stroke oil, for example, shows little money is likely to have been spent elsewhere on essential maintenance.

Restoration photographs
If the scooter has been restored, then there will normally be a photographic record, of some type – no matter how haphazard. Make sure that the scooter you're looking at is actually the one in the photos. Look at areas where recent work can be easily verified. Ask the seller for copies of the photos, as they will be just as valuable to you, in the future.

Import papers
The appeal of buying an unregistered import has tarnished recently with the introduction in the UK of the NOVA (Notification of Vehicle Arrival) system. Every import has to be assessed by HM Revenue and Customs, and given a clearance number, before the DVLA will register the scooter, whether it comes from the EEC or farther afield. There are lots for sale on the internet which have not gone through this system, and these should be avoided, or a hefty discount arranged to compensate for having to sort out all the paperwork. In addition, make sure, if you buy an import, that all numbers match any official documents that came with it, to avoid any other bureaucratic nightmares.

12 What's it worth?
– let your head rule your heart

Having worked your way through the inspection chapters of the book, you should now have a very good idea of the condition of your prospective purchase. Whether it's a total basket case, a tidy scooter ready to use straight away, or one of the many states in between, its value to you isn't necessarily solely related to its structural and mechanical condition. Other factors, such as rarity and desirability, have an impact, too. The time and money needed, to bring a '80s PX125 up to your desired level may not be reflected in its market value; but the same amount, spent on an original SS 90, would most certainly be money well spent.

Geared Vespas were, almost always, fairly austere machines. Originally designed to get Italians mobile at the cheapest price, trim and other luxuries were often ignored. That situation didn't last long; a thriving aftermarket sector quickly grew, offering a bewildering range of bolt-on goodies, to make your scooter go faster, look better, or simply carry more. These little extras can now be worth a fortune, with certain accessories making up a sizeable percentage of the asking price for the scooter they're attached to.

Looks fabulous, and if you find one covered in original '60s fittings, worth a lot of money.

Customising splits opinion, and reduces the potential market if you want to sell later.

Less universally acceptable is tuning and customising. Buying a heavily modified Vespa is a risky option, as the desirability of any changes is subjective. This is particularly true for older machines, upgraded to modern specifications. To the dismay of purists, many VBBs have had 8 inch wheels replaced by 10 inch, and a PX 200cc engine bolted-in. Whether this is the correct way to treat one of, a now dwindling number, of original scooters is open to debate. Long-term (and solely concentrating on value) the market for these scooters will probably decline, as purity of form holds sway over function. A similar loss in later resale value may be experienced with restored, or rejuvenated machines (depending on the choice of colour).

These issues are not easily quantifiable, so once you've decided how much, or little, weight you give them, in choosing your purchase, the final consideration is; are you willing to haggle? Use some of the defects you'll have, undoubtedly, found during the examination process as leverage to get a price reduction. If the seller is stubborn, it may not work – but it costs nothing to try. Beware wading in with an unjustifiably low starting offer, or you could risk alienating the seller altogether; at least try to look reasonable. If the seller won't budge on price, ask if they have a workshop manual, or any service parts you can have. Dealers may be the most flexible on price, as they'll have inflated the price to begin with (to cover possible warranty work or rectify minor problems, pre-sale).

13 Do you really want to restore?
– it'll take longer and cost more than you think

Usually, in the world of classic vehicles, restoration is only financially viable if you're able to do all the work yourself, and you're applying those skills to one of the rarer, more valuable variants. At first glance, the world of classic Vespas appears to very much back this theory, with a plethora of restored machines available, at temptingly low prices. But as usual, if something appears too good to be true, it usually is. Many of these machines originate in the Far East, and their refurbishment can be deeply flawed (unless purchased from a reputable supplier). There are several reported cases of frames being made by welding together two or three others (known as 'cutting and shutting' in the back-street car repair world). This can seriously weaken the whole structure. Engines are often assembled with worn parts, damaged cases welded up, or otherwise bodged together – even basics, such as wheel and fork bearings, badly worn. If you would like one of these scooters, speak to Vespa club members; get recommendations on who to buy from – but search the internet for horror stories about these scooters, and what to look out for, before finally deciding to part with your money.

Restore it, or ride it just as it is?

UK restored scooters are, usually, much better; just double check that all the work was done here. It's always worth asking others who have used the shop recently, as even the best can have bad patches. Ask to see recent examples of their work – and still carry out the checks in this book – times are hard, and the temptation to cut the odd corner may have proved too tempting to ignore. Well established dealers, who have been trading for many years, have a hard-earned reputation to uphold, and are definitely the best bet.

Assuming, then, that you'd be willing to restore a Vespa yourself (rather than risk buying a potentially dodgy one), is it viable? Suitable project scooters still turn up regularly, but prices in Italy and Spain, where they remain plentiful, have risen sharply recently, and the

If you want detailing like this, make sure your restorer is up to the job.

quality has dropped. Before you start the whole process, be ruthless about your own abilities. Will you be able to cut-out, and then weld-in, a floor repair section? Will your paintwork be up to scratch? Have you ever stripped and rebuilt an engine? All these skills can be achieved by most people, but do you have the time and inclination to gain them? Have you got the necessary tools, or enough scootering friends who could lend them to you?

If you answered negative to the above questions, try a quick price calculation. To have the frame dipped or blasted, then have the jobs above done professionally, and adding in likely parts costs, you'll have a ball park figure. Experience shows this will probably end up being around half the final total. The figure-juggling is up to you, and very much depends on the state of the scooter to begin with. The only unquantifiable part, is the amount of satisfaction you'll have at the end of it all – plus the peace of mind in knowing that it has all been done correctly. If someone else is doing the work, make sure that you're very clear when specifying what needs to be done. For example: if you want a paint job, are you paying for a flat off, spot, prime, and blow over? Or are you expecting a full, bare metal respray? Whatever you've agreed with your chosen repairer, get it down on paper – particularly the price. The quotation should also include a reference along the lines of: 'The final cost will not exceed the quoted figure by more 10 per cent'. The last place you want a surprise is on the final bill. This might all seem a bit negative, but there is nothing more disheartening than seeing a project stalled, in the corner of the garage, due to lack of money or interest. Have a look in the adverts of any scootering magazine, there will probably be loads of 'unfinished projects' on offer; you really don't want your dream to end up that way, as it usually involves losing money as well.

14 Paint problems
– bad complexion, including dimples, pimples and bubbles

This chapter gives you some idea of the most common paint problems you may encounter – and what you'd need to do to sort them out, if you can't live with them. In most cases, rectification is expensive.

Fading
A common problem, particularly with reds. This afflicts all shades that have lived in sunnier climes, so expect Italian imports to have bleached paint. T-Cut restoring compound may work, but if the surface is too far gone, a repaint is the only option. The problem can also crop-up if a poor quality, low-pigment paint was used to respray; or at the edges of a repair, where paint has been blown in to part of a panel.

Remove a side panel and you may be able to see the degree of paint fade.

Bubbling
This is a result of sub-surface rust. Usually, only 10% of the problem is visible; thin threads of corrosion will be running across the metal, next to the bubbling scab, under apparently sound paint. The only solution is to find – and kill – all the rust, and then repaint. Bubbling can also show up where filler is applied over old rust; the corrosion continues to grow, forcing the filler away from the metal.

Crazing/cracking
Crazing and cracking go hand-in-hand; the result of poor surface preparation before painting. It can also be caused by panel damage (such as creasing) after a bump or fall. The only

Flaking can also start from years of exposure to the sun, or a knock.

cure is to strip the paint back to bare metal, clean, prime, and re-coat. Dissimilar paints, applied during patch repairs, can also cause crazing. On scooters with a clear coat, applied over the base colour, the lacquer often peels at the edges of a panel, or around stone chips.

Orange peel
This is easy to spot, as the paint surface resembles the skin of an orange, with an obvious, lumpy texture. This is caused by the topcoat being applied too thickly. In this case though, a good depth of paint is fortunate; you can often flat the surface with fine grade wet-and-dry, then buff back to a level, shiny finish.

Hopefully, you'll never come across orange peel quite this bad.

Micro blistering
These tiny blisters are caused by water or solvent, left on the surface before the topcoat was applied. Unfortunately, apart from taking the paint back to a sound surface and starting again, there's little you can do.

Micro blistering exposes the primer beneath.

Silicone dimples
Another sub-surface problem, resulting from poor preparation, or a lack of cleanliness where applying the paint. The paint settles on tiny balls of silicone or grease, rather than flowing evenly over the surface. It then dries in small, dished craters. Once again, the only cure is to remove the paint, degrease the metal, and start again.

Stone chips
These are really irritating, as corrosion spreads rapidly if not promptly addressed. Vespa legshields, and the generously proportioned front mudguards, seem to attract this type of damage. Touch-up sticks can be used successfully, as long as the correct shade can be found (Fiat colours are often a good match).

15 Problems due to lack of use
– just like their owners, scooters need exercise!

Engine problems
If left sitting for too long, piston rings can seize in the bore. A top end strip, and a new set of rings, is a wise precaution for anything that's been left for more than a couple of years – even if the motor isn't locked up. Bearings can corrode when not in use, and clutch plates stick, as the oil drains off. Crankcase seals stick to the crank, tearing slightly when turned, after a long period standing.

Hydraulic problems
Brake fluid is hygroscopic (it attracts water from the atmosphere), causing internal corrosion to brake components. Calipers, in particular, stick – although master cylinders are not immune. Bleed nipples can become stuck, so they snap off at the slightest provocation.

Calipers – and pads – seize, as hydraulic fluid absorbs moisture.

Electrical problems
Batteries die if left uncharged for any length of time, as particles held in suspension during use drop to the bottom, shorting out the plates (replacement being the only solution). Electrical connectors corrode, causing all sorts of problems. After long periods of inactivity, charging systems often develop faults, soon after being pressed into service.

Stale fuel
This is a real problem. Modern, unleaded fuel, deteriorates far more quickly than the older, leaded variety. This is compounded if the scooter is a pre-autolube model (where the oil is mixed-in), as it separates out, over time, forming a semi-liquid goo. Jets can gum-up, and even petrol tanks corrode, internally, above the fuel line. If the Vespa was stored for any length of time, the owner should have, first,

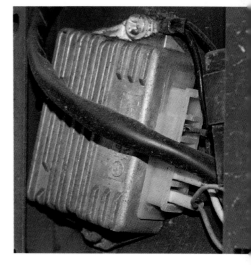

All electrical components suffer when left, even solid-state ones.

Vespa cables eventually seize-up, even in use; leaving them only accelerates the process.

Exhaust systems are rot-prone, from inside and out.

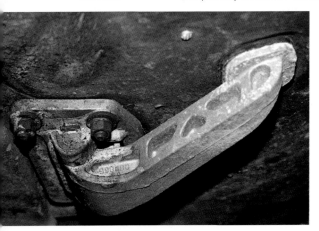

left the engine running, with the fuel tap turned off, before being put away. (This ensures the carburettor is empty.) If the fuel tap has been left on (and the carb needle-valve is in less than perfect condition) petrol can seep past the valve, into the crankcases and gearbox. If used in this condition, the gearbox will be severely damaged. If the cylinder fills, hydraulic locking can bend the conrod.

Tyres

These have a finite life of around 5 years (even less if they're left under inflated, or in direct sunlight). The treads may seem fine, but the compound is likely to have hardened with age (so check the sidewalls for cracking). Rear tyres can also develop flat spots, as they're permanently under pressure from the weight of the engine unit.

Control cables

Cable servicing is often ignored, when the scooter is in use, so when left, they quickly stiffen up or seize. Oiling might help, but replacement is the most likely long-term solution.

Exhaust

Vespa exhausts are not long lasting. The insides rot, due to internal condensation (produced by all petrol fuelled vehicles). This destroys the baffles, as well as the casing; a decline dramatically accelerated by being left for long periods. Shorter periods of inactivity can still cause problems; oil residue can harden, and partially block the exhaust, causing power loss, and increasing fuel consumption.

Brakes

Brake shoe operating cams can stick in the backplates. Footbrake pivots stick (especially the later, under-floor type), and disc pads seize in their caliper slots – all of which can cause brake binding, or a lack of efficiency.

Brake pedal pivot-pins seize-up

16 The Community
– key people, organisations and companies in the Vespa world

UK clubs
Vespa Club of Great Britain
www.vespaclubofbritain.co.uk
Email: membershipsecretary@
vespaclubofbritain.co.uk
Veteran Vespa Club
www.veteranvespaclub.com
Email: membership@veteranvespaclub.
com
Vintage Motor Scooter Club
www.vmsc.co.uk
Email: info@vmsc.co.uk

European clubs
Austria
Vespa Club Austria
www.vespaclub.at
Belgium
Vespa Club Belgium
www.vespaclub.be
Croatia
Vespa Club Croatia
www.vespaclubcroatia.com
France
Vespa Club France
www.vespaclubdefrance.fr
Germany
Vespa Club Germany
www.vcvd.de
Greece
Vespa Club Greece
www.vespaclub.gr
Holland
Vespa Scooter Club Netherlands
www.vespascooterclubnederland.nl

Israel
Vespa Club Israel
www.israeli-vespa.org
Italy
Vespa Club Italy
www.vespaclubditalia.it
Poland
Vespa Club Poland
www.vespaclub.org.pl
Portugal
Vespa Clube Portugal
www.vespaclubeportugal.pt
Serbia
Vespa Club Serbia
www.vespaclubsrbija.rs
Spain
Vespa Club Spain
www.vespania.es
Switzerland
Vespa Club Switzerland
www.rollerclub.ch

USA, Canada, Australia and New Zealand clubs
USA
Vespa Club of America
www.vespaclubusa.org
Canada
Vespa Club of Canada
www.vespaclubofcanada.com
Australia
Vespa Riders Club of Australia
www.facebook.com/Vespa-Riders-Club-of-Australia

The suppliers and specialists listed below represent just a small sample of outlets in their respective countries. Inclusion is not a recommendation, and please treat any obvious omissions as accidental. The best solution is to talk to other owners, in your area, for up-to-date information on the best businesses to satisfy your requirements. Don't forget your local scooter shop, as they can provide useful information, too, as well as sell you parts.

UK parts suppliers
Allstyles Scooters
www.allstyles-scooters.com
Beedspeed
www.beedspeed.com
Buzz Solomoto
www.buzzsolomoto.co.uk
Ron Daley Scooters
www.rondaleyscooters.co.uk
PM Tuning
www.pmtuning.co.uk
Readspeed
www.readspeedscooters.com
Retrospective Scooters
www.retrospectivescooters.com
Scooter Products
www.scooterproducts.com
Scooterworks
www.scooterworks-uk.com
Solely Scooters
www.solelyscooters.co.uk
A J Sutton
www.ajsutton.co.uk
VE UK
ww.malossiuk.com

Continental and worldwide parts suppliers
Australia
GPS Imports
www.gpsimports.com.au
Belgium
Vespa Classic Parts
www.vespaclassicparts.com
France
Scooter World
www.scooterworld.fr
Vintage Scooter Service
www.vintagescooter.com
Germany
SIP Scootershop
www.sipscootershop.com
Italy
Vespa Vintage Parts (Genuine Piaggio)
www.vespavintageparts.com
Scooter Vintage
www.scootervintage.it
RMS Classic
www.classic.rms.it
New Zealand
Vespa Spares
www.vespaspares.co.nz
Spain
SOLO MOTO
www.recambiomoto.com
USA
Scooterworks
www.scooterworks.com
Scooter West
www.scooterwest.com
American Scooter Centre
www.americanscootercentre.com
Scooters Originali
www.scootersoriginali.com
Vietnam
ScootRS
www.scootrs.com
Saigon Scooter Centre
www.saigonscootercentre.com

Books

History
60 Years of the Vespa
Haynes
ISBN 978-1844253135
Giorgi and Santi
Vespa An Illustrated History
Haynes
ISBN 978-1844256808
Brockway and Henshaw
Vespa From Italy with Love
Nada Italia
ISBN 978-8879112222
Biancalana and Marchiano
Vespa
Rizzoli International
ISBN 978-0847829361
Valerio Boni

Technical
Vespa PX125 / 150 / 200cc Workshop Manual
Haynes
ISBN 978-1844253890
Shoemark and Mather
Vespa 90,125,150,180,200cc Workshop Manual
Haynes
ISBN 978-0856961267
Jeff Clew
How to Restore your Vespa Motor Scooter
Motorbooks International
ISBN 978-0760306239
Darnell and Golfen

Living with a vespa
Vroom with a view
Bantam Books
ISBN 978-0553816372
Peter Moore www.petermoore.net
Vroom by the Sea
Summersdale
ISBN 978-1840247374
Peter Moore

Magazines

UK
Scootering
www.scootering.com
Classic Scooterist Scene
www.scooteristscene.com

DVD
In Search of Vespa
Delta Leisure Group
www.deltamusic.co.uk
55 minutes
Vespa Running Maintenance
Scooter Techniques
www.scootertechniques.co.uk
150 minutes
Vespa Engine Rebuild
Scooter Techniques
www.scootertechniques.co.uk
300 minutes

www.velocebooks.com / www.veloce.co.uk
All current books • New book news • Special offers • Gift vouchers

17 Vital statistics
– essential data at your fingertips

These figures are from Piaggio documents. Top speeds look a little conservative, whereas fuel consumption figures look better than most riders would expect; but they do serve as a comparison.

The sixties
SS90
6bhp @ 6000rpm
77kg
93kph max (58mph)
2.6 litre per 100km (108mpg)

150 GL
6bhp @ 5000rpm
97kg
90kph (56mph)
2.4 litre per 100km (117mpg)

The seventies
125 Primavera
5.6bhp @ 5500rpm
76kg
88kph (55mph)
2 litre per 100km (140mpg)

Rally 200
12.5bhp @ 5700rpm
106kg
110kph (68mph)
2.8 litre per 100km (100mpg)

The eighties
125PX
8bhp @ 5600rpm
80kg
95kph (59mph)
3 litre per 100km (93mpg)

125PX T5
11bhp @ 6700rpm
110kg
108kph (67mph)
2.7 litre per km (103mpg)

The nineties onward
PX200 Disc
11bhp @ 6000rpm
115kg
110kph (68mph)
2.8 litre per 100km (100mpg)

PX125 Catalytic
8.3bhp @ 6000rpm
115kg
90kph (56mph)
2.4 litre per 100km (117mpg)

Vespa timeline

1946 The first Vespas hit the streets. A 98cc two-stroke, with a rod gear change, and a mudguard mounted headlamp. Approximately 2,500 were sold, in the first year.

1948 A 125cc model arrives, with spring suspension for greater comfort.

1951 Cables replaced the rod change; a massive improvement.

1953 Internal engine changes gave more power and better economy.

1954 150cc model arrives, with a handlebar mounted headlight. Speedos were now standard.

1955 The GS150 is launched. 150cc engine, with a four speed box. As fast as similar capacity motorcycles, it was highly desirable.

1956 One million Vespas had been produced.

1957 The handlebars are replaced with a cast headset, giving the style that would endure until the end of production.

1958	Frame changes are made to simplify production.
1959	Rotary valve induction arrives; a major mechanical step forward.
1960	Two million scooters have rolled down the production line.
1963	GL model; with trapezoid headlight, and other styling changes, it proves to be a very popular model. The small frame Vespa hits the market; small size and small capacity – aimed squarely at the youth market.
1965	The sporting SS90, with its highly individual styling, is launched.
1967	Primavera enters the fray, remaining on sale, virtually unchanged, for 15 years.
1968	Rally 180 gives rotary valve induction to the sporting Vespas.
1969	50 Special, with rectangular headlight, and finned drums, maintains the sales success of the small frames.
1970	Four million Vespas have been made.
1972	Rally 200 brings electronic ignition to the showroom; a great export success.
1976	ET3, with improved three-port motor, gives the 125 small frame a power boost.
1977	200PE. Top of the range, and worthy of that position; a great upgrade, all round, but with '80s styling.
1978	125 / 150PX follows its big brother onto the market.
1982	The PK range, with its (unfortunately) bulky styling, is thrust upon an unwilling public.
1985	PX125 T5. Adds a performance option to the bottom end of the range.
1996	Piaggio celebrates its 50th anniversary, with over 15 million scooters sold.
1997	All PX models receive front disc brakes.
1999	Emissions laws catch up with the Vespa; a catalytic converter is fitted, to the detriment of performance.
2002	A much improved instrument panel is added.
2008	The PX comes to the end of the road, having been the best selling Vespa model ever.
2011	They thought it was all over ... but Piaggio managed to tinker with the old PX and bring it up to Euro 3 emissions standards, so once again a two stroke Largeframe is available to buy brand new.

The Essential Buyer's Guide™ series ...

978-1-845840-22-8

978-1-845840-26-6

978-1-845840-29-7

978-1-845840-77-8

978-1-845840-99-0

978-1-904788-70-6

978-1-845841-01-0

978-1-845841-19-5

978-1-845841-13-3

978-1-845841-35-5

978-1-845841-36-2

978-1-845841-38-6

978-1-845841-46-1

978-1-845841-47-8

978-1-845841-63-8

978-1-845841-65-2

978-1-845841-88-1

978-1-845841-92-8

978-1-845842-00-0

978-1-845842-04-8

978-1-845842-05-5

978-1-845842-70-3

978-1-845842-81-9

978-1-845842-83-3

978-1-845842-84-0

978-1-845842-87-1

978-1-84584-134-8

978-1-845843-03-8

978-1-845843-09-0

978-1-845843-16-8

978-1-845843-29-8

978-1-845843-30-4

978-1-845843-34-2

978-1-845843-38-0

978-1-845843-39-7

978-1-845841-61-4

978-1-845842-31-4

978-1-845843-07-6

978-1-845843-40-3

978-1-845843-48-9

978-1-845843-63-2

978-1-845844-09-7

... don't buy a vehicle until you've read one of these!

978-1-845843-52-6   978-1-845846-55-8   978-1-845847-55-5   978-1-845843-54-0   978-1-845843-92-2   978-1-845843-59-5   978-1-845843-60-1

978-1-845847-56-2   978-1-845843-77-9   978-1-845843-91-5   978-1-845844-42-4   978-1-845845-23-0   978-1-845843-95-3   978-1-845844-08-0

978-1-845844-21-9   978-1-845844-22-6   978-1-845844-23-3   978-1-845844-24-0   978-1-845844-30-1   978-1-845844-34-9   978-1-845845-25-4

978-1-845844-43-1   978-1-845844-45-5   978-1-845844-47-9   978-1-845844-56-1   978-1-845844-62-2   978-1-845848-06-4   978-1-845844-87-5

978-1-845845-26-1   978-1-904788-69-0   978-1-845845-33-9   978-1-904788-72-0   978-1-904788-85-0   978-1-845846-09-1   978-1-845844-86-8

978-1-904788-98-0   978-1-845845-71-1   978-1-845846-14-5   978-1-845841-07-2

£9.99-£12.99 / $19.95-$25.00
(prices subject to change, p&p extra).

For more details visit
www.veloce.co.uk or email info@veloce.
co.uk

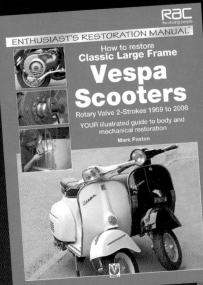

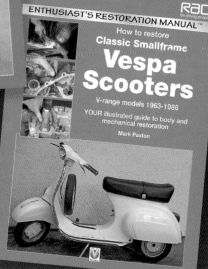

Index